# TREASURES *of* WOMANHOOD

# TREASURES of WOMANHOOD

## Timeless Words of Faith and Inspiration

Compiled by

SUSAN EVANS McCLOUD

Cover painting *The Letter* © William Whitaker

Published by Covenant Communications, Inc.
American Fork, Utah



Printed in the United States of America
First Printing: April 1999

06 05 04 03 02 01 00 99 10 9 8 7 6 5 4 3 2 1

ISBN 1-57734-447-2

# Contents

## *The Mystery & the Magnificence*

So God created man in his own image, in the image of God created he him; male & female created he them . . . And Adam said, This is now bone of my bones, and flesh of my flesh: she shall be called **Woman,** because she was taken out of Man.

— GENESIS 1:27, 2:23

The especial genius of women I believe to be electrical in movement, intuitive in function, spiritual in tendency.

— MARGARET FULLER

Diversity is strength, not a division. . . . When white light falls on a wall, it makes a white wall. But when it passes through a prism, that same light makes a rainbow.

— *CHIEKO N. OKAZAKI

Please know that I am aware of the hazards. I want to do it because I want to do it. Women must try to do things as men have tried. When they fail, their failure must be but a challenge to others.

— AMELIA EARHART

*Note: Each name preceded by an asterisk (*) indicates a woman of the Latter-day Saint faith.

A liberated woman is one who feels confident in herself, and is happy in what she is doing. She is a person who has a sense of self . . . It all comes down to freedom of choice.

— BETTY FORD

I feel weak, but I will rely on my Heavenly Father, for I know He will bless my feeble efforts, for He has said, "Unto thy day, thy strength shall be."

— *DR. ELLIS REYNOLDS SHIPP

I had an early run in the woods before the dew was off the grass . . . I sang for joy, my heart was so bright and the world so beautiful . . . It seemed as if I *felt* God as I never did before, and I prayed in my heart that I might keep that happy sense of nearness all my life.

— LOUISA MAY ALCOTT

God answers sharp and sudden on some prayers,
And thrusts the thing we have prayed for in our face, A gauntlet with a gift in't.

— ELIZABETH BARRETT BROWNING

The Soul selects her own Society—
Then—shuts the Door—
To her divine Majority—
Present no more . . .

— EMILY DICKINSON

For years I have endeavoured to calm an impetuous tide—labouring to make my feelings take an orderly course—it was striving against the stream.

— MARY WOLLSTONECRAFT

Behind every great man is an exhausted woman.

— LADY SAM FAIRBAIRN

Four be the things I'd be better without:
Love, curiosity, freckles, and doubt.

— DOROTHY PARKER

For there is no friend like a sister
In calm or stormy weather;
To cheer one on the tedious way,
To fetch one if one goes astray,
To lift one if one totters down,
To strengthen whilst one stands.

— CHRISTINA ROSSETTI

So many gods, so many creeds,
So many paths that wind and wind,
While just the art of being kind
Is all the sad world needs.

— ELLA WHEELER WILCOX

Religion is love; in no case is it logic.

— BEATRICE WEBB (NEE POTTER)

When women go wrong, men go right after them.

— MAE WEST

The happiest women, like the happiest nations, have no history.

— GEORGE ELIOT (MARY ANN EVANS)

As I read of the great spirituality of women of the past and realize how the Lord communicated with them, I thrill with the spiritual manifestations that accompanied their missions in life, literally a power of evidencing the will of God made known through their instrumentality. I think of Eliza R. Snow, of whom Joseph F. Smith said, "She walked not in the borrowed light of others, but faced the morning unafraid and invincible."

—*ARDETH GREENE KAPP

Love, which is only an episode in the life of a man, is the entire history of woman's life.

— MME. DE STAEL

No coward soul is mine,
No trembler in the world's storm-troubled sphere:
I see Heaven's glories shine,
And faith shines equal, arming me from fear.

— EMILY BRONTË

When I see the elaborate study and ingenuity displayed by women in the pursuit of trifles, I feel no doubt of their capacity for the most herculean undertakings.

— JULIA WARD HOWE

We are tomorrow's past.

— MARY WEBB

The best woman has something of a man's strength; and the noblest man of a woman's gentleness.

— MISS MULOCK

The basic discovery about any people is the discovery of the relationship between its men and its women.

— PEARL S. BUCK

There is always a "but" in this imperfect world.

— ANNE BRONTË

She keeps on being queenly in her own room with the door shut.

— EDITH WHARTON

When a woman behaves like a man, why doesn't she behave like a nice man?

— DAME EDITH EVANS

If I ever felt inclined to be timid as I was going into a room full of people, I would say to myself, "You're the cleverest member of one of the cleverest families in the cleverest class of the cleverest nation in the world, why should you be frightened?"

— BEATRICE WEBB

Shyness is just egotism out of its depth.

— PENELOPE KEITH

How reconcile this world of fact with the bright world of my imagining? My darkness has been filled with the light of intelligence, and behold, the outer day-light world was stumbling and groping in social blindness.

— HELEN KELLER

You must try not to mind growing up into a pretty woman.

— JANE AUSTEN

All generations of women
who ground the flour for bread,
And set it by their ovens,
and curved strong hands to knead,
How intimately they knew
whence man's true symbols come:
The seed, the yeast, the bread,
the child swelling in the womb.

— NANCY FLORENCE KEESING

Grandma Alcott came to visit us. A sweet old lady; and I am glad to know her, and see where Father got his nature. Eighty-four; yet very smart, industrious, and wise. A house needs a grandma in it.

— LOUISA MAY ALCOTT

Where so many hours have been spent in convincing myself that I am right, is there not some reason to fear I may be wrong?

— JANE AUSTEN

For all the churches you can build, and all the books you can export, will never do much good without what a gentleman in that Colony very appropriately called "God's police" — wives and little children — good and virtuous women.

— CAROLINE CHISHOLM

All my life through, the new sights of Nature made me rejoice like a child.

— MARIE CURIE

I have not written for days because life has been too full. And now there are only scraps left — nice ones and disagreeable ones. I don't like living too fast to savor it, too fast to be conscious. Conscious only that one is wasting it on trivialities for the most part and not putting it into anything that counts.

— ANNE MORROW LINDBERGH

It is a trite but true saying that "there is no excellence without great labor." God virtually says to each of us, *The world is before you; be as good and as great as you will, and I will assist you.*

— *ROMANIA PRATT PENROSE

Woman gives her hand, her heart, her all to her husband, *she gives herself.* The apex of her hopes is one whom she can love and honor as her head, one who is wise and judicious and is governed, and governs, by the pure principles of the gospel.

— *DR. ELLIS REYNOLDS SHIPP

The state of the world today demands that women become less modest and dream/plan/act/risk on a larger scale.

— CHARLOTTE BUNCH

It is probably true to say that the largest scope for change still lies in men's attitude to women, and in women's attitude to themselves.

— VERA BRITTAIN

Yes, I am wise, but it's wisdom full of pain,
Yes, I've paid the price, but look how much I've gained, I am wise, I am invincible, I am Woman.

— HELEN REDDY

The prolonged slavery of women is the darkest page in human history.

— ELIZABETH STANTON

Women have always been the guardians of wisdom and humanity, which makes them natural, but usually secret, rulers. The time has come for them to rule openly, but together with and not against men.

— CHARLOTTE WOLFF

Some women want to be men . . . I never felt that way. I was always glad that I was a girl, a woman, a wife, a mother. This is our mission, the greatest work that we can perform in this life is to be true wives and faithful mothers. Greater joy could not be had.

— *DR. ELLIS REYNOLDS SHIPP

Women are expected to do twice as much as men in half the time and for no credit. Fortunately, this isn't difficult.

— CHARLOTTE WHITTON

It takes a soul to move a body:
It takes a high-souled man to move the masses,
Even to a cleaner style:
It takes the ideal to blow a hair's-breadth
Off the dust of the actual.

— ELIZABETH BARRETT BROWNING

Woman's work! Housework's the hardest work in the world. That's why men won't do it.

— EDNA FERBER

The cock croweth but the hen delivereth the goods.

— ANONYMOUS

Women are door-mats and have been —
The years those mats applaud —
They keep their men from going in
With muddy feet to God.

— MARY CAROLYN DAVIES

Then give to the world the best you have, and the best will come back to you.

— *MARY AINGE DEVERE

Spring rides no horses down the hill,
But comes on foot, a goose girl still,
And all the loveliest things there be
Come simply so, it seems to me. . .

— EDNA ST. VINCENT MILLAY

Life isn't long enough to do all you could accomplish. And what a privilege even to be alive. In spite of all the pollutions and horrors, how beautiful this world is. Supposing you only saw the stars once every year. Think what you would think. *The wonder of it!*

— TASHA TUDOR

There's One above who watches o'er us all,
Who even hears the lonely ravens cry,
He notes each little sparrow if it fall,
And to the humble He is ever nigh.

— *EMMELINE B. WELLS

God does not send strange flowers every year.
When the spring winds blow o'er the pleasant places,
The same dear things lift up the same fair faces.

— ADELINE DUTTON TAIN

I will not let you say a woman's part
must be to give exclusive love alone;
Dearest, although I love you so, my heart
answers a thousand claims besides your own.

— ADELAIDE ANNE PROCTER

Life and its few years —
A wisp of fog betwixt us and the sun.

— LIZETTE WOODWORTH REESE

I refuse to consign the whole male sex to the nursery. I insist on believing that some men are my equals.

— BRIGID BROPHY

I'm furious about the Women's Liberationists. They keep getting up on soapboxes and proclaiming that women are brighter than men. That's true, but it should be kept very quiet or it ruins the whole racket.

— ANITA LOOS

Women have a way of treating people more softly. We treat souls with kid gloves.

— SHIRLEY CAESAR

Every day is a fresh beginning,
Every morn is the world made new.

— SARAH CHAUNCEY WOOLSEY

Women have served all these centuries as looking-glasses possessing the magic and delicious power of reflecting the figure of man at twice its natural size.

— VIRGINIA WOOLF

Women are repeatedly accused of taking things personally. I cannot see any other honest way of taking them.

— MARYA MANNES

Supposing you have tried and failed again and again. You may have a fresh start any moment you choose, for this thing that we call "failure" is not the falling down—but the staying up.

— MARY PICKFORD

My last act in that precious spot was to tidy the rooms, sweep up the floor, and set the broom in its accustomed place behind the door. Then with emotions in my heart which I could not now pen and which I then strove with success to conceal, I gently closed the door and faced an unknown future, faced a new life, a greater destiny as I well knew — but I faced it with faith in God.

— *BATHSHEBA SMITH
(UPON LEAVING NAUVOO)

Risk! Risk anything! Care no more for the opinions of others, for those voices. Do the hardest thing on earth for you. Act for yourself. Face the truth.

— KATHERINE MANSFIELD

I have seen Mother magnificent before,
but usually it has been a kind of personal thing.
Here she was herself, and yet not herself.
She was humble.
And in this humility before her mission—
the carrying on of what she believed in (education
for women)—she was magnificent.
She had reached a kind of peak in her life.
She had reached that moment all scholars,
scientists, saints and artists strive for. I was . . .
happy for her, and proud of her.

— ANNE MORROW LINDBERGH

If you decide to play it safe in life you've decided that you don't want to grow any more.

— SHIRLEY HUPSTEDLER

I've got a woman's ability to stick to a job and get on with it when everyone else walks off and leaves it.

— MARGARET THATCHER

Woman must come of age by herself. . . . She must learn not to depend on another, nor to feel she must prove her strength by competing with another. In the past, she has swung between these two opposite poles of dependence and competition, of Victorianism and Feminism. Both extremes throw her off balance; neither is the center, the true center of being a woman. She must find her true center alone. She must become whole . . . she must . . . follow the advice of the poet to become "world to oneself for another's sake."

— ANNE MORROW LINDBERGH

To the lovers and the dreamers and enthusiasts it is sometimes given to move the world with their shoulder; the plodders do it stone by stone, while the ages admire their patience. The last are like schoolboys learning, but to the first the heavens and hells have whispered.

— MRS. W. K. CLIFFORD

A thousand unseen hands reach down to help you to their heights, and all the forces of the firmament shall fortify your strength. Be not afraid to thrust aside half-truths and grasp the whole.

— ELLA WHEELER WILCOX

I've lived long enough now to know that the whole truth is never told in history texts. Only the people who lived through an era, who are the real participants in the dream as it occurs, know the truth. The people of each generation, it seems to me, are the most accurate historians of their time.

— LILLIAN GISH

Because we cannot solve our own problems right here at home, we talk about problems out there in the world. Can one make the future a substitute for the present? And what guarantee have we that the future will be any better if we neglect the present?

— ANNE MORROW LINDBERGH

Do not imagine a good woman is satisfied with virtue's own reward. The consciousness of her own worth is not sufficient to keep her happy if you are silent and never seek to impress upon her mind the fact that you realize her good qualities. And this is especially true if you take every opportunity to assure her that you see her faults.

— ELLA WHEELER WILCOX

If a woman is sufficiently ambitious, determined *and* gifted—there is practically nothing she can't do.

— HELEN LAWRENSON

Because of their age-long training in human relations—for that is what feminine intuition really is—women have a special contribution to make to any group enterprise.

— MARGARET MEAD

I walke manie times . . . into the pleasant fieldes of the Holye Scriptures, where I pluck up the goodlie greene herbes of sentences, eate them by reading, chewe them up by musing, and laie them up at length in the seate of memorie . . . so I may the lesse perceive the bitterness of this miserable life.

— QUEEN ELIZABETH I

Silence ruled this land. Out of silence mystery comes, and magic, and the delicate awareness of unreasoning things.

— ELEANOR DARK

The world is young, and you must take
Your making, breaking, shaping way.

— ROSEMARY DOBSON

'Tis sweet to love. I think indeed it is to those who love most, who are most Godlike. Not the base and groveling passion that the world calls love, but love pure and chaste, based upon the intrinsic attributes of the soul. This is the kind of love that satisfies my nature, and may I ever be worthy of it.

— *DR. ELLIS REYNOLDS SHIPP

One doesn't recognize in one's life the really important moments—not until it's too late.

— DAME AGATHA CHRISTIE

A prophetess? Yea, I say unto you, and more than a prophetess—an uncommon pretty young woman.

— GEORGE ELIOT

People do not live nowadays—they get about ten percent out of life.

— ISADORA DUNCAN

Give me your tired, your poor,
Your huddled masses yearning to breathe free,
The wretched refuse of your teeming shores,
Send these; the homeless, tempest-tossed, to me:
I lift my lamp beside the golden door.

— EMMA LAZARUS
(VERSE INSCRIBED ON THE STATUE OF LIBERTY)

"It may well be," said Cadfael, "that our justice sees as in a mirror image, left where right should be, evil reflected back as good, good as evil, your angel as her devil. But God's justice, if it makes no haste, makes no mistakes."

— ELLIS PETERS

More and more it appears that, biologically, men are designed for short, brutal lives and women for long, miserable ones.

— ESTELLE RAMEY

There are no ugly women, only lazy ones.

— HELENA RUBINSTEIN

They the royal-hearted women are
Who nobly love the noblest, yet have grace
For needy suffering lives in lowliest place,
Carrying a choicer sunlight in their smile,
The heavenliest ray that pitieth the vile.

— GEORGE ELIOT

Woman's grief is like a summer storm,
Short as it is violent.

— JOANNA BAILLIE

Our deeds still travel with us from afar,
And what we have been makes us what we are.

— GEORGE ELIOT

A woman's rank
Lies in the fulness of her womanhood:
Therein alone she is royal.

— GEORGE ELIOT

Freedom's daughter, rouse from slumber:
see, the curtains are withdrawn,
Which so long thy mind hath shrouded,
Lo! thy day begins to dawn.
Truth and virtue be thy motto,
temperance, liberty and peace;
Light shall shine and darkness vanish,
Love shall reign, oppression cease.

— *LULU GREENE RICHARDS

Began the study of blood, chemically. How interesting and delightful are my studies. I used to think the study of medicine so dry and obtuse, and how erroneous were my impressions! I think that it causes everything in nature to be fraught with greater interest. How happy must be a thoroughly educated person, for even the cursory knowledge I have gained in the last few months has opened to my view depths and heights of which I had never dreamed.

— *DR. ELLIS REYNOLDS SHIPP

"Unless I keep the island-quality intact somewhere within me, I will have little to give to my husband, my children, my friends or the world at large. . . Woman must still be the axis of a wheel in the midst of her activities; she must be the pioneer in achieving this stillness, not only for her own salvation, but for the salvation of family life, of society, perhaps of our civilization.

— ANNE MORROW LINDBERGH

# LOVE:

## *The Flowering of a Woman's Soul*

There is no fear in love;  
but perfect love casteth out fear . . .  
He that feareth is not made perfect in love.

— 1 JOHN 4:18

She had this inward happiness, for she had Christopher to love her, to comfort her, to feed her with sweet names: and she flowered in his warmth into a beauty she had never possessed . . . obviously what the world needed was love. She couldn't help thinking this when she caught sight of her own changed face in the glass.

— ELIZABETH VON ARNIM

I need your love as a touchstone of my existence. It is the Sun which breathes life into me.

— JULIETTE DROUET TO VICTOR HUGO

Man is the slave of the kiss. With a kiss a woman can tame the wildest man. By a kiss the strongest man's will becomes soft as wax.

— JOACHINDA BELLAY

Love is a great beautifier.

— LOUISA MAY ALCOTT

You are my sympathy—my better self—my good angel—I am bound to you with a strong attachment. I think you are good, gifted, lovely: a fervent, a solemn passion is conceived in my heart; it leans to you, draws you to my center and spring of life, wraps my existence about you—and, kindling in pure, powerful flame, fuses you and me in one.

— CHARLOTTE BRONTË

I would rather have a crust and a tent with you than be queen of all the world.

— ISABEL BURTON

TO HER EXPLORER HUSBAND, RICHARD

A [marriage] relationship is tried and tested in times of disappointment, discouragement, and maybe even despair. But when we link arms and tread the way to God, hand in hand, the valleys that we traverse together can bring us to the mountain peaks . . . Love isn't something we store up. We draw it fresh from God each day. The love that we express can feed the soul of both the one who gives and the one who receives. It can become a message of power to transform lives because, in expressing true love, we must dip into the reservoir of divine love, the love of Christ. We share in part the pure love of Christ, the fountain of all love.

—*ARDETH GREENE KAPP

Now she seemed merry as a lark; in her lover's genial presence, she glanced like some soft glad light. How beautiful she grew in her happiness.

— CHARLOTTE BRONTË

If, in the Eternal Plan, woman should be led, it should be a capable leadership. My ideal of the union of the sexes I had found in the blessed union of my parents, for they were indeed "two souls with but a single heart; two hearts that beat as one." Never in their lives was there the arrogance of domination. How I praise the Eternal Father for this sublime example, this pattern for carrying on life's purposes, our Creator's sacred command for mortal companionship, a union divine . . . which lasts through all the eternities of time.

— *DR. ELLIS REYNOLDS SHIPP

To my dear husband . . . I give this manuscript of a work which would never have been written but for the happiness which his love has conferred on my life.

— GEORGE ELIOT, THE ENGLISH NOVELIST,
TO GEORGE LEWES, WITH WHOM
SHE LIVED UNTIL HIS DEATH,
BUT NEVER MARRIED

His kisses touch her marveling eyes
And wander searching through her thinking face;
And though so loved and near she lies . . .
He knows he travels in a distant place.

— VIOLA MEYNELL

I do not love thee!— no! I do not love thee!
And yet when thou art absent I am sad:
And envy even the bright blue sky above thee,
Whose quiet stars may see thee and be glad.

— CAROLINE NORTON

Oh! to feel I was, and am, loved by such an Angel as Albert was too great delight to describe! he is perfection; perfection in every way—in beauty—in everything! I told him I was quite unworthy of him and kissed his dear hand . . . I really felt it was the happiest, brightest moment in my life, which made up for all I had suffered and endured.

— FROM THE JOURNAL OF QUEEN VICTORIA

Best and kindest of all that ever were to be loved in dreams, and wondered at and loved out of them, you are indeed! . . . I may say before God and you, that of all the events of my life, inclusive of its afflictions, nothing has humbled me so much as your love. . . . Your love has been to me like God's own love, which makes the receivers of it kneelers.

— ELIZABETH BARRETT TO ROBERT BROWNING

To her love was like the air of heaven—invisible, intangible; it yet encircled her soul, and she knew it; for in it was her life.

— MISS M'INTOSH

Love is not just a nice feeling about someone. It is the pure and joyful pulse of the universe, and being in tune with it means you are in tune with the forces that bind together the stars on one hand and the atoms on the other.

—*CHIEKO N. OKAZAKI

My soul was darker than midnight, when your pen said, "Let there be light," and there was light as at the bidding of the Word . . . Oh, my dearest Friend! be always so good to me, and I shall make the best and happiest Wife. When I read in your looks and words that you love me, I feel it in the deepest part of my soul; then I care not one straw for the whole Universe beside.

— JANE WELSH TO THOMAS CARLYLE

The soul of a woman lives in love.

— MRS. SIGOURNEY

The woman who has not touched the heart of a man before he leads her to the altar, has scarcely a chance to charm it when possession and security turn their powerful arms against her.

— MRS. COWLEY

Love for me was always—is always—waiting, watching, longing, a test of patience and endurance. A perpetual learning and humbling and something held in, that you had to learn how to give wisely and well. . . . A whole science, loving is, an art. A dedication. One has to train oneself for it, discipline oneself to it, perhaps throughout a whole lifetime.

— ANNE MORROW LINDBERGH

Love is the virtue of women.

— MME. DUDEVANT

To love one who loves you, to admire one who admires you, in a word, to be the idol of one's idol, is exceeding the limit of human joy—it is Stealing Fire from Heaven.

— MME. DE GIRARDIN

Must love be ever treated with profaneness, as a mere illusion? or with coarseness, as a mere impulse? or with fear, as a mere disease? or with shame, as a mere weakness? or with levity, as a mere accident? whereas it is a great mystery and a great necessity, lying at the foundation of human existence, morality, and happiness—mysterious, universal . . . inevitable as death.

— HARRIET MARTINEAU

Why is it so difficult to love wisely—
so easy to love too well?

— MISS M. E. BRADDON

Love never reasons, but profusely gives; gives, like a thoughtless prodigal, its all, and trembles then lest it has done too little.

— HANNAH MORE

Among all the many kinds of first love, that which begins in childish companionship is the strongest and most enduring; when passion comes to unite its force to long affection, love is at its spring-tide.

— GEORGE ELIOT

However dull a woman may be, she will understand all there is in love; however intelligent a man may be, he will never know but half of it.

— MME. FEE

One hour of love will teach a woman more of her true relations than all your philosophizing.

— MARGARET FULLER

Joy is a net of love by which you can catch souls.

— MOTHER TERESA

The air is blowing in my ears,
and music echoes just above it,
I smile at the waiting books,
pretending they can replace you.
But pauses always come to pretenders.
And suddenly I am with you:
In your dreams, or down the street you walk.
I cannot put what hasn't passed behind.

— SALLY SEWELL

Most women set out to try to change a man, and when they have changed him, they do not like him.

— MARLENE DIETRICH

A woman cannot love a man she feels to be her inferior; Love without veneration and enthusiasm is only friendship.

— MME. DUDEVANT

Weep not that thou hast grown tired of me. I am strengthened by your sorrow, and ever I stand by, and wait, to fill the gap that has so newly sprung between us. Time will heal, and you will let me wipe your tears away, and I shall press my lips against your mournful eyes.

— MAE MARTIN

Where love and wisdom drink out of the same cup, in this every-day world, it is the exception.

— MME. NECKER

These, our dark days, have lived because of you,
How many times I've drunk your love and praise
As one who thirsts and cannot ever fill!
But in my highest moments when I thrill
To the best love and knowledge I possess,
I love you—with such purity and joy!

— *SUSAN EVANS MCCLOUD

Love is the purification of the heart from itself; it strengthens and ennobles the character, gives higher motive and nobler aim to every action of life, and makes both man and woman strong, noble, and courageous. . . . The power to love truly and devotedly is the noblest gift with which a human being can be endowed; but it is a sacred fire that must not be burned to idols.

— MISS JEWSBURY

And if a heart is sore with sting
From slight or words unkind,
May I the balm of solace bring,
Their wounds to soothe and bind.
Oh, help me love humanity,
And all its virtues see,
For those who love most tenderly
Are surely most like Thee.

— *DR. ELLIS REYNOLDS SHIPP

People talk about love as though it were something you could give, like an armful of flowers. Love is a force in you that enables you to give other things. It is a motivating power.
It enables you to give strength and power, freedom and peace to another person.
It is not a product—it produces!
It is a power—like money or electricity.
It is valueless unless you can give something else by means of it.

— ANNE MORROW LINDBERGH

All the privilege I claim for my own sex . . . is that of loving longest, when existence or when hope is gone.

— JANE AUSTEN

Love is the loadstone of love.

— MRS. OSGOOD

I never thought this would bring me as much satisfaction as success, fame and money—that being married to an Australian, living in a suburb of Sydney, and having a child would be particularly satisfying. But I love it! I find it much more rewarding than getting parts in films.

— RACHEL WARD

I have loved hours at sea, gray cities,
    The fragile secret of a flower,
Music, the making of a poem
    That gave me heaven for an hour;

First stars above a snowy hill,
    Voices of people kindly and wise,
And the great look of love, long hidden,
    Found at last in meeting eyes.

— SARA TEASDALE

Beauty is altogether in the eye of the beholder.

— MARGARET WOLFE HUNGERFORD

I paint a picture in my mind of you,
And try to pretend that
I'm only interested in the color scheme . . .
They tell me the stories
That have no ending,
And I suppose I will use them
To paint my life . . .
If only I could paint the sunset . . . or the tide
Upon an empty shore.

— MORAG MCCLOUD

All love that has not friendship for its base is like a mansion built upon the sand,
Though brave its walls as any in the land; yet, when from the frowning east a sudden gust
Of adverse fate is blown, or sad rains fall; day in, day out, against its yielding wall,
Lo! the fair structure crumbles to the dust. Love, to endure life's sorrows and earth's woe,
Needs friendship's solid masonwork below.

— ELLA WHEELER WILCOX

Taught from their infancy that beauty is woman's sceptre, the mind shapes itself to the body, and roaming round its gilt cage, only seeks to adorn its prison.

— MARY WOLLSTONECRAFT

A man is seldom ashamed of feeling that he cannot love a woman so well when he sees a certain greatness in her: nature having intended greatness for men.

— GEORGE ELIOT

Already the second day since our marriage;
his love and gentleness is beyond everything,
and to kiss that dear soft cheek,
to press my lips to his, is heavenly bliss.
I feel a purer, more unearthly feeling than I ever did.
Oh! was ever woman blessed as I am.

— QUEEN VICTORIA (FROM HER JOURNALS)

Wild Nights—wild nights! Were I with thee
Wild Nights should be our Luxury!
Futile the Winds—To a Heart in port—
Done with the Compass—Done with the Chart!
Rowing in Eden—Ah, the Sea!
Might I but Moor—Tonight—In Thee.

— EMILY DICKINSON

His beautiful courtesy was never more in evidence than when he approached any one of his wives whom he loved and who loved him. Especially was that so when in the company of Mother Young . . . to her he paid exquisite attention, quiet, composed, but sincere. His attitude of consideration towards her was reflected in that of every other wife and child he had.

— *SUSA YOUNG GATES
(OF HER FATHER, BRIGHAM YOUNG)

She bore about with her, she could not help knowing it, the torch of her beauty; she carried it erect into any room that she entered; and after all, veil it as she might, and shrink from the monotony of bearing that it imposed on her, her beauty was apparent. She had been admired. She had been loved.

— VIRGINIA WOOLF

A woman despises a man for loving her, unless she returns his love.

— ELIZABETH DREW STODDARD

When we are young, she thought, we worship
romantic love for the wrong reasons . . .
and, because of that, subsequently repudiate it.
Only later, and for quite other reasons,
we discover its true importance.
And by then it has become tiring even to observe.

— SHIRLEY HAZZARD

The average man is more interested in a woman who is interested in him than he is in a woman—any woman—with beautiful legs.

— MARLENE DIETRICH

I don't think men and women were meant to live together. They are totally different animals.

— DIANA DORS

It is only the women whose eyes have been washed clear by tears who get the broad vision that makes them little sisters to all the world.

— DOROTHY DIX

After all, my erstwhile dear, my no longer cherished,
Need we say it was not love, just because it perished?

— EDNA ST. VINCENT MILLAY

Lord, grant your mercy unto me:
Teach me some way that he may know
My love for him is not an empty show,
But purest tenderness and constancy.

— MARY, QUEEN OF SCOTS

A woman dictates before marriage in order that she may have an appetite for submission afterwards.

— GEORGE ELIOT

The woman who loves should indeed be the friend of the man she loves; she should heed not her selfish and often mistaken desires, but his interest whose fate her own interest inspires. And rather than seek to allure, for her sake, his life down the turbulent, fanciful wake of impossible destinies, use all her art that his place in the world finds its place in her heart.

— *SUSA YOUNG GATES

In February Father came home. A dramatic scene when he arrived in the night. We were waked by hearing the bell. Mother flew down, crying "My husband!" We rushed after . . . May said, after he had told all the pleasant things, "Well, did people pay you?" Then, with a queer look he opened his pocket-book and showed one dollar, saying with a smile that made our eyes fill, "Only that!" . . .

I shall never forget how beautifully Mother answered him, though the dear, hopeful soul had built much on his success; but with a beaming face she kissed him, saying, "I call that doing *very well.* Since you are safely home, dear, we don't ask anything more." Anna and I choked down our tears, and took a lesson in real love which we never forgot— nor the look that the tired man and the tender woman gave one another.

— LOUISA MAY ALCOTT

My husband came, my heart gave one great bound towards him; O how enthusiastically I love him; truly and devotedly. If he could only feel towards me in any degree as I do towards him, how happy it would make me.

— *EMMELINE B. WELLS

God has implanted in the human heart a principle or sentiment which calls for companionship. "It is not good for man to be alone," was pronounced when our first parents were placed upon the earth. Surrounded as he was by everything that seemed desirable, yet the Creator of it all knew his happiness could not be complete if left in loneliness. . . . It is as natural for you girls to desire a husband, a home, as it is for you to breathe . . . The main point of interest to us is that we bestow our love upon a worthy object and then prove ourselves of equal worth.

— *JULIA A. MACDONALD

I will be so excited to see him . . . I will be filled with longings and frustrations. His coming will fill the house with warmth, with fire, with wind, with life. And also with problems. . . . What *time* marriage takes—but it is life. It would be death without it.

— ANNE MORROW LINDBERGH

For the mother is and must be, whether she knows it or not, the greatest, strongest and most lasting teacher her children have.

— HANNAH WHITALL SMITH

A mother holds her children's hands for awhile—
their hearts forever.

— ANONYMOUS

A mother's heart, like primroses, opens
most beautifully in the evening of life.

— ANONYMOUS

One of the ways we can prepare to be in the family circle of God's household is to establish a home as nearly like His as we can.

—*BARBARA B. SMITH

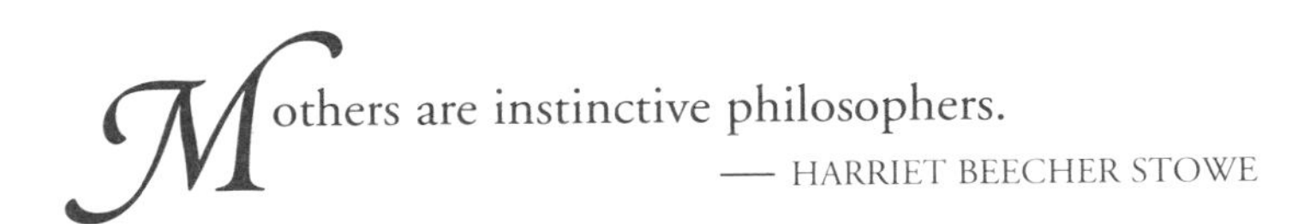

Mothers are instinctive philosophers.

— HARRIET BEECHER STOWE

Sometimes the poorest woman leaves her children the richest inheritance.

— RUTH E. RENKEL

Men want only to improve the world;
but mothers want to improve their whole family.
That is a much harder task.

— ANONYMOUS

I've become a mother. That's why women grow up, and men don't.

— KATHLEEN CLEAVER

Furnish an example. Stop preaching, stop shielding, don't prevent self-reliance and initiative—allow your children to develop along their own lines.

— ELEANOR ROOSEVELT

I long to put the experience of fifty years at once into your young lives, to give you at once the key of that treasure chamber every gem of which has cost me tears and struggles and prayers. But you must work for these inward treasures yourselves.

— HARRIET BEECHER STOWE

There was a beautiful ideal in your mind:
I saw it; that was my mother!

— SOPHIA HAWTHORNE

A child is fed with milk and praise.

— MARY LAMB

Mothers bear a great responsibility. But guilt is a burden they need not pick up. They need not make themselves responsible for the deficiencies of society. It is not for them to bear unmerited guilt for divorce, juvenile delinquency, drug abuse, teenage sexuality, theft, and violence. They need to know where they stand in their own eyes and where they stand with the Lord. That precious knowledge is not something they should let someone else decide for them.

—*CHIEKO N. OKAZAKI

"Mother"—a word that holds the tender spell
Of the dear essential things of earth.

— GRACE NOLL CROWELL

Giving advice comes naturally to mothers. Advice is in the genes along with blue eyes and red hair.

— LOIS WYSE

I cannot recall what happened during the first months after my illness. I only know that I sat in my mother's lap or clung to her dress as she went about her household duties . . . My mother succeeded in making me understand a good deal. I always knew when she wished me to bring her something, and I would run upstairs or anywhere else she indicated. Indeed, I owe to her loving wisdom all that was bright and good in my long night.

— HELEN KELLER

God knew that everybody needs
someone to show the way,
He knew that babies need
someone to care for them each day . . .
He knew they needed someone sweet
to soothe their baby cries,
To teach them how to walk and talk,
and sing them lullabies . . .
That's why God made mothers.

— KATHERINE NELSON DAVIS

What is a mother? Who shall answer this?
A mother is a font and spring of life,
A mother is a forest in whose heart
Lies hid a secret ancient as the hills,
For men to claim and take its wealth away;
And, like the forest, shall her wealth renew
And give, and give again, that men may live.

— FRANCIS CARDINAL SPELLMAN

A mother is not a person to lean on—but a person to make leaning unnecessary.

— DOROTHY FISCHER

In the beginning there was my mother. A shape. A shape and a force, standing in the light. You could see her energy; it was visible in the air. Against any background she stood out.

— MARILYN KRYSL

There are unnumbered women who have "mothered" children who are not their own . . . Mother is a title that belongs to every woman by lineage from our earliest mother, Eve—and also by eternal destiny.

—*BARBARA B. SMITH

Mighty is the force of motherhood! It transforms all things by its vital heat.

— GEORGE ELIOT

Thou straggler into loving arms,
Young climber up of knees,
When I forget thy thousand ways,
Then life and all shall cease.

— MARY LAMB

Blessed Dear, and Heart's Delight,
Companion, Friend and Mother mine,
Round whom my fears and love entwine.

— CHRISTINA ROSSETTI

Sometimes the strength of motherhood is greater than natural laws.

— BARBARA KINGSOLVER

Your mother loves you like the deuce while you are coming. Wrapped up there under her heart is perhaps the cosiest time in existence. Then she and you are one: companions.

— EMILY CARR

I know not how to part, with tolerable ease, from the little creature.

— MARY ROWLANDSON

You who are darkness warmed my flesh,
where out of darkness rose the seed.
Then all a world I made in me:
all the world you hear and see
hung upon my dreaming blood.

— JUDITH WRIGHT

I begin to love this little creature, and anticipate his birth as a fresh twist to a knot, which I do not wish to untie.

— MARY WOLLSTONECRAFT SHELLEY

My life reshapes in your tiny unfinished hands . . .
I swell to the size of your life . . .
Keep me this way as long as you want.

— SUSAN TAYLOR

You can spend so much time with children! I don't do anything all day except be with the baby—see what he wants, watch him learn and discover himself. And yet I'm so tired at night—It's like coming from thirty hours of steady work.

— SOPHIA LOREN

A well-ordered home is my chief delight, and the affectionate domestic wife with the Relative Duties which accompany that character my highest ambition.

— ABIGAIL ADAMS

There are people who say the lives of women are narrow. They are not narrow. They are as wide as sympathy and as broad as love . . . a person may encircle the globe with mind open only to bodily comfort. Another may live his life on a sixty-foot lot and listen to the voices of the universe.

— BESS STREETER ALDRICH

The Crown of the house is Godliness.
The Beauty of the house is Order.
The Glory of the house is Hospitality.
The Blessing of the house is Contentment.

— OLD INSCRIPTION

Like being in love with a lover, being in love with a child colors things. You aren't to be trusted. Everything is a bit more than it seems. Everything seems a bit more than it is.

— BARBARA ASCHER

. . . there's so much more. You and I, child, have just begun. Think: worlds from now what might we be? —We, who are seed of Deity.

— *CAROL LYNN PEARSON

If there be aught surpassing human deed or word or thought, it is a mother's love!

— MARCHIONES DE SPADARA

All the earth, though it were full of kind hearts, is but a desert place to a mother when her only child is absent.

— ELIZABETH GASKELL

Some are kissing mothers and some are scolding mothers — but it is love just the same, and most mothers kiss and scold together.

— PEARL S. BUCK

Women do not have to sacrifice personhood if they are mothers. They do not have to sacrifice mother-hood in order to be persons.

— ELAINE HEFFER

Now, as always, the most automated appliance in a household is the mother.

— BEVERLY JONES

My dear mother, a prototype, awake and alert—each morning found her with a smiling face and willing hands caring for her household, her plans all made beforehand, her precious time budgeted for each meal to be prepared, the number of skeins of yarn she would spin, the stockings she would darn, the buttons to sew on, the clothing to be mended, her hours for the garden, wash days, soap-making days, candles to be moulded, times for dyeing her skeins, even her bread-making and dishwashing all scheduled so that when the frugal evening meal was over and every performance cleared up, she was ready for the rest and joy of the beautiful evening hour. Then, while her husband read to her or the two conversed, she with still-busy fingers created pretty laces to adorn her children's clothing, to decorate her household furnishings, curtains and valances, table cloths and pillow slips . . . for indeed in those days those skillful hands were never found idle in her waking hours.

— *DR. ELLIS REYNOLDS SHIPP

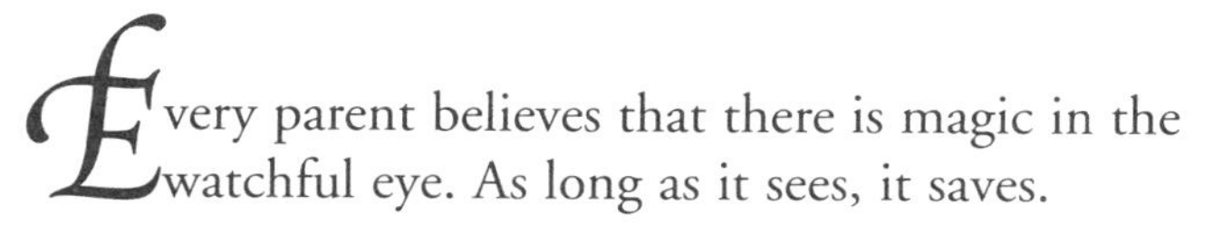

Every parent believes that there is magic in the watchful eye. As long as it sees, it saves.

— BARBARA ASCHER

Family faces are magic mirrors. Looking at people who belong to us, we see the past, present and future.

— GAIL BUCKLEY

There is in all this cold and hollow world no fount of deep, strong, deathless love, save that within a mother's heart.

— MRS. HEMANS

The mother's yearning . . . feels the presence of the cherished child even in the base, degraded man.

— GEORGE ELIOT

The strength of a nation, especially of a republican nation, is in the intelligent and well-ordered homes of the people.

— MRS. SIGOURNEY

Everybody's mother still cares.

— LILLIAN HELLMAN

Oh to go back to childhood, to days of innocent youth,
To confident reliance, to its trusting love and truth.
And oh to commence anew at the fount that maketh clean,
The o'erburdened heart renew with the light of hope within.
To find joy in each season, breathe of the pure, balmy air;
Roam 'mong beauties of nature, free from the thraldom of care.
In childhood's hopeful morning, untaught in the ways of men.
Unskilled in worldly wisdom, be a free, glad child again.

— *LULU GREENE RICHARDS

A strong man can make a woman over into anything in the world he desires her to be, if he will go about it with the same perseverance and determination which he puts into his business . . . And remember always—the real business of life is the making of a happy home. Everything else is secondary to that; for, when you come to sift the whole chaff of existence, everything goes to the winds but the happiness we have had at home.

— ELLA WHEELER WILCOX

Whatever beauty or poetry is to be found in my little book is owing to your interest in and encouragement of all my efforts from the first to the last; and if ever I do anything to be proud of, my greatest happiness will be that I can thank you for that, as I may do for all the good there is in me; and I shall be content to write if it gives you pleasure.

— LOUISA MAY ALCOTT (TO HER MOTHER)

Four children—only an excuse? But if you walk away from them and leave them entirely to the nurse you don't know them and their problems. There are so many things only a mother can know or do. Writing comes out of life; life *must* come first.

— ANNE MORROW LINDBERGH

I taught the winter term at Driggs for the munificent sum of $35.00 per month. With my consent, at the end of almost every month Mother would come down after my check on payday to buy feed for the stock. I was glad to let her have it. It made me very proud to be able to help the family out. I taught for twenty-five years.

— *MARY HULET COBURN

Take my hand, child, there are dangers at our feet,
And I see them all: Take my hand, child—lest I fall.

— *CAROL LYNN PEARSON

Mother, my love for you is more than last year's love,
Deeper, more tender, for I have seen my heart
Laid bare to pain and fear I never knew—uncertainties.
And then I thought of you—who did endure,
Who somehow still possess a vernal faith, a singing
gentleness.
I see new things, harmonious and fair, More of you,
Mother—
The you that was always there.

— *SUSAN EVANS MCCLOUD

I'll keep a little tavern belong the high hill's crest,
Wherein all grey-eyed people may sit them down to rest.
There shall be plates a-plenty, and mugs to melt the chill
Of all the grey-eyed people who happen up the hill.

There sound will sleep the traveller, and dream his
journey's end,
But I will rouse at midnight the falling fire to tend.
Aye, 'tis a curious fancy—but all the good I know
Was taught me out of two grey eyes a long time ago.

— EDNA ST. VINCENT MILLAY

Are not the mothers of every race and color the custodians of the physical development and health of their people? . . . How few mothers realize the effect of their own mental condition upon the minds of their offspring. How soon the little innocent face learns to smile when mamma smiles, to beam with delight when she is happy, and look sad and try to wipe the tears away with its tiny hand when sadness and tears are on her face. And likewise when swayed by the stronger and more tempestuous emotions of anger, hate, or fear do these tender ones partake, to a very great extent, of the same sensation.

— *DR. ELLIS REYNOLDS SHIPP

Oh, wondrous power! how little understood, entrusted to the mother's mind alone, to fashion genius, form the soul for good, inspire a West, or train a Washington.

— MRS. HALE

Backward, flow backward, O tide of the years!
I am so weary of toil and of tears;
Toil without recompense, tears all in vain;
Take them, and give me my childhood again!
I have grown weary of dust and decay,—
Weary of flinging my soul wealth away;
Weary of sowing for others to reap;—
Rock me to sleep, mother,—rock me to sleep!

— ELIZABETH AKERS ALLEN

God sends children for another purpose than merely to keep up the race—to enlarge our hearts; and to make us unselfish and full of kindly sympathies and affections; to give our souls higher aims; to call out all our faculties to extended enterprise and exertion; and to bring round our firesides bright faces, happy smiles, and loving, tender hearts.—My soul blesses the great Father, every day, that he has gladdened the earth with little children.

— MARY HOWITT

As I sat down by Saddle Stream
to bathe my dusty feet there,
A boy was coming up the hill
any girl would meet there.
As I went over Woody Knob
and dipped into the hollow,
A youth was coming up the hill
any maid would follow.
Then in I turned at my own gate—
and nothing to be sad for—
To such a man as any wife
would pass a pretty lad for!

— EDNA ST. VINCENT MILLAY

Often into folly straying, O, my mother!
how I've grieved her!
Oft I've heard her for me praying,
till the gushing tears relieved her;
And she gently rose and smiled,
whispering, "God will keep my child."

— MRS. F. D. HEMANS

Did you ever hear my mother sing?
'Tis the sweetest, softest note
That ever quivered on the air,
or rose from human throat.
How oft upon my bed I've lain,
when racked with pain and woe,
Bereft of rest and worn with grief,
such grief as women know . . .
Thus to my bedside mother came,
and with her accents mild,
She soothed and lulled and rested me,
her suffering, sleepless child.
O Mother, thy dear voice would fail
to please a critic's ear,
Yet when thy songs are gently raised,
I feel the angels near . . .
And sweeter far than all the rest
my mother's song inspires,
A pure and hallowed memory
of heaven and heavenly choirs.

— *SUSA YOUNG GATES

This book is all that's left me now —
tears will unbidden start —
With faltering lips and throbbing brow
I press it to my heart.
For many generations past here is our family tree;
My mother's hands this Bible clasped,
she, dying, gave it me.
My father read this holy book to brothers, sisters, dear;
How calm was my poor mother's look who loved
God's word to hear!
Her angel face — I see it yet!
What thronging memories come!
Again that little group is met within the walls of Home!

— MARY MORRIS

Childhood has no forebodings: but then it is soothed by no memories of outlived sorrow.

— GEORGE ELIOT

# The Cardinal Virtues

For intelligence cleaveth unto intelligence; wisdom receiveth wisdom; truth embraceth truth; virtue loveth virtue; light cleaveth unto light; mercy hath compassion on mercy and claimeth her own.

— D&C 88:40

# Appreciation

To love one that is great, is almost to be great oneself.

— MME. NECKAR

No story is the same to us after a lapse of time; or rather we who read it are no longer the same interpreters.

— GEORGE ELIOT

Those who make us happy are always thankful to us for being so; their gratitude is the reward of their benefits.

— MME. SWETCHINE

Next to invention is the power of interpreting invention; next to beauty the power of appreciating beauty.

— MARGARET FULLER

Isn't it the most blessed moment — the return home! If I were a cat, I would purr with gratitude on these ecstatic homecomings.

— TASHA TUDOR

We dance with the daughters of morning. Their unheard strains nurture the sacred lyrics of our lives . . . and all things dark and common part for us.

— *SUSAN EVANS MCCLOUD

God wove a web of loveliness,
of clouds and stars and birds,
But made not anything at all
so beautiful as words.

— ANNA HEMPSTEAD BRANCH

Earth's crammed with heaven,
And every common bush afire with God;
But only he who sees, takes off his shoes.

— ELIZABETH BARRETT BROWNING

O world, I cannot hold thee close enough!
Thy winds, thy wide grey skies!
Thy mists, that roll and rise!
Thy woods, this autumn day, that ache and sag
And all but cry with colour! That gaunt crag
To crush! To lift the lean of that black bluff!
World, World, I cannot get thee close enough!
Long have I known a glory in it all,
But never knew I this:
Here such a passion is
As stretcheth me apart,—Lord, I do fear
Thou'st made the world too beautiful this year;
My soul is all but out of me,—let fall
No burning leaf; prithee, let no bird call.

— EDNA ST. VINCENT MILLAY

The few primitive pictures I had chanced to see whetted my desire for more—"The Boys Purloining the Farmer's Apples" and "The Country Maid." These pictures, with just a few others—all I could enjoy outside of those nature had painted.

— *DR. ELLIS REYNOLDS SHIPP

Life never becomes a habit to me—it is always a marvel.

— KATHERINE MANSFIELD

Morning is glad on the hills. The sky sings in blue tones. Little blue fleurs are early blooming now. I do so like blue. When I grow up I am going to write a book about the glads of blue. The earth sings in green.

— OPAL WHITELEY

If God is love, the source, the spring,
should not the lover
Pilgrimage there—reverently seeking supply?—
That the cup he gives will not be dry.

— *CAROL LYNN PEARSON

I saw the spires of Oxford
As I was passing by,
The grey spires of Oxford
Against a pearl-grey sky:
My heart was with the Oxford men
Who went abroad to die. . . .

They left the peaceful river,
The cricket field, the quad,
The shaven lawns of Oxford,
To seek a bloody sod.
They gave their merry youth away
For country and for God.

God rest you, happy gentlemen,
Who laid your good lives down,
Who took the khaki and the gun
Instead of cap and gown.
God bring you to a fairer place
Than even Oxford town.

— WINIFRED M. LETTS

# Benevolence

He who has never denied himself for the sake of giving, has but glanced at the joys of charity.

— MME. SWETCHINE

He who will not give some portion of his ease, his blood, his wealth, for others' good, is a poor frozen churl.

— JOANNA BAILLIE

Sow good services; sweet remembrances will grow from them.

— MME. DESTAEL

What do we live for, if it is not to make life less difficult to each other?

— GEORGE ELIOT

A poor man served by thee, shall make thee rich.

— ELIZABETH BARRETT BROWNING

We are rich only through what we give,
And poor only through what we refuse and keep.

— MME. SWETCHINE

I shall not pass this way again—
Then let me now relieve some pain,
Remove some barrier from the road,
Or brighten some one's heavy load;
A helping hand to this one lend,
Then turn some other to befriend.

— EVA ROSE YORK

The weather is damp and cloudy. Mary and Eddie Tanner are boarding with us going to school. They have been home to Payson and came back about noon. Mary said, "Who has been in my room and left the wash bowl dirty?" But she did not say, "Who has swept and dusted so nicely, and put up clean curtains to make it nice and pleasant?" It is human nature. How much quicker we are to find fault and speak of what annoys us than of that which is pleasant and cheerful.

— *MARY JANE TANNER

We are bound not only to do, but to feel, toward others as we would have others feel toward us. . . . The command implies something more than mere honesty; it requires charity as well as integrity.

— EMMA EMBURY

We hand folks over to God's mercy, and show none ourselves.

— GEORGE ELIOT

True worth is in *being,* not *seeming,*
in doing, each day that goes by,
Some little good—not in dreaming
of great things to do by and by.
For whatever men say in their blindness,
and spite of the fancies of youth,
There's nothing so kingly as kindness,
and nothing so royal as truth.

— ALICE CARY

I am strong again—today I gave, and forced my own anxieties aside, and bared my heart to beauty and to love, and listened to the sounds of my own soul; today I gave — and found my own heart whole.

— *SUSAN EVANS MCCLOUD

Had the pleasure of providing Marmee with many comforts, and keeping the hounds of care and debt from worrying her. She sits at rest in her sunny room, and that is better than any amount of fame to me.

— LOUISA MAY ALCOTT

Mother, I wish I could kneel at your feet today and look into your beautiful eyes, as deep as wells, as piercing as an arrow, as tender as a wild rose petal, and caress your hands, those magic hands. Eight times you have come to my bed to bring me safely through the "valley of shadow." You always knew just how to hold my back so it wouldn't hurt so much, and no matter how your own back might have been aching—it wasn't too much to give all of your strength to me.

— *ELLIS SHIPP OF HER DOCTOR MOTHER,
ELLIS REYNOLDS SHIPP

What comes next for willing hands to do? My councilors and I wallowed through the snow until our clothes were wet a foot high to get things together, give out notices, etc. We pieced blocks, carded bats, quilted, and got together 27 quilts, besides a great amount of other clothing, for the needy.

— *LUCY MESERVE SMITH

I did have thinks as how I would stop to get watercress for the mama on the way home from school. She does have such a fondness for it. And, too, she does have longings for singing lessons. All the pennies that the man that wears grey neckties and is kind to mice does give to me I save. I have nineteen pennies, and when I grow up I am going to buy her a whole rain barrel of singing lessons.

— OPAL WHITELEY

# Character

How shall we estimate the power of example; the influence which we exert upon the lives of others! . . . Many true and earnest souls are, by their patient self-sacrifices, their devotion to truth, their cheerfulness under adverse circumstances, their sympathy and benevolence, making of their lives the most eloquent poems which, we doubt not, are being written by the angels on the tablets above, and when the books shall be opened, and the records read, they will be found to be rich in a harvest of noble results.

— *SUSA YOUNG GATES

If I take care of my character, my reputation will take care of itself.

— MRS. MOODY

Conventionality is not morality. Self-righteousness is not religion. To attack the first is not to assail the last. To pluck the mask from the face of the Pharisee, is not to lift an impious hand to the Crown of Thorns.

— CHARLOTTE BRONTË

"Character," says Novalis, in one of his questionable Aphorisms—"character is destiny."

— GEORGE ELIOT

One of the greatest lessons the Savior taught is that boundaries exist to be crossed . . . What do we do with differences? Do they paralyze us, or can they become part of the beauty of our lives? . . . Only when we get close do we really know the inner heart of the individual . . . We have to discover a person's inside, patiently and lovingly. We have to learn to love other people by serving them.

—*CHIEKO N. OKAZAKI

Those who would reform the world must show that they do not speak in the heat of wild impulse; their lives must be unstained by passionate error; they must be severe lawgivers to themselves.

— MARGARET FULLER

I want, by understanding myself, to understand others. I want to be all that I am capable of becoming.

— KATHERINE MANSFIELD

Now that John is dead, I can truly say we all had cause to bless the day he came into the family; for we gained a son and brother, and Anna the best husband ever known. For ten years he made her home a little heaven of love and peace; and when he died he left her the legacy of a beautiful life, and an honest name to his little sons.

— LOUISA MAY ALCOTT

It is while a person stands undecided, uncommitted, and uncovenanted, with choices waiting to be made, that vulnerability to every wind that blows becomes life-threatening. Uncertainty, the thief of time and commitment, breeds vacillation and confusion. It is in taking a stand and making a choice to follow our leaders that we become free to move forward. We are then released from the crippling position of doubtful indecision and confusion. We then have access to power and influence—so much so that we can hardly keep pace with our opportunities.

—*ARDETH GREENE KAPP

Discipline is the whole lesson that we have come down on this earth to learn . . . Hasty words, selfish acts, uncharitable thoughts must be governed and controlled. The whole life must be lived, not to please and satisfy the loves and lusts of the flesh, but to bring the body under subjection of the spirit. Oh, this valuable, lovely lesson!

— *SUSA YOUNG GATES

The voice of conscience is so delicate that it is easy to stifle it; but it is also so clear that it is impossible to mistake it.

— MME. DE STAEL

And so my spirits rise again, with praise and sustenance. I ought to so maintain myself—with my own faith and pride; I ought to carry sustenance inside.

— *SUSAN EVANS MCCLOUD

The mind will ever be unstable that has only prejudices to rest on.

— MARY WOLLSTONECRAFT

Believe not those who say the upward path is smooth, lest thou should stumble on the way and faint before the truth.

— ANNE BRONTË

Let us look for the Savior in the eyes and faces of those around . . . "The glory of the Lord and the excellency of our God" is all around us—in the world that he has created for us, in the faces of others, and in ourselves. We know the way. Jesus said, "I am the way." Let us follow him, rejoicing, and enter Zion with singing.

—*CHIEKO N. OKAZAKI

# Duty

The reward of one duty done is the power to fulfil another.

— GEORGE ELIOT

There is nothing in the universe that I fear, but that I shall not know all my duty, or shall fail to do it.

— MARY LYON

Reverence the highest; have patience with the lowest; let the day's performance of the meanest duty be thy religion.

— MARGARET FULLER

There are not good things enough in life, to indemnify us for the neglect of a single duty.

— MME. SWETCHINE

Can any man or woman choose duties? No more than they can choose their birthplace, or their father and mother.

— GEORGE ELIOT

The virtues, like the Muses, are always seen in groups. A good principle was never found solitary in any breast.

— JANE PORTER

The million little things that drop into our hands, the small opportunities each day brings He leaves us free to use or abuse and goes unchanging along His silent way.

— HELEN KELLER

O Lord, give me thy spirit that it may be a light to my path; give me knowledge that I may know Thy will and how to do it; give me wisdom that I may judge between truth and error, for I desire to do good and not evil. Make the path of duty plain before me—and give me grace to walk therein.

— *PATTY SESSIONS

# FAITH

It is faith among men that holds the moral elements of society together, as it is faith in God that binds the world to His throne.

— MRS. KIRKLAND

He who would undermine the foundations of our hope for eternity, seeks to beat down the column which supports the feebleness of humanity.

— MRS. NEVINS

He that loses hope may part with anything.

— MRS. LEE

I never saw a moor, I never saw the sea;
Yet know I how the heather looks,
and what a wave must be.
I never spoke with God, nor visited in heaven;
Yet certain am I of the spot as if the chart were given.

— EMILY DICKINSON

O, tell not of the heroines of olden time, but think of those who've lived in modern days, whose fortitude and faith, proven in deeds sublime, deserve remembrance, commendation, praise. Crossing the Mississippi river, frozen o'er, bidding Nauvoo a long and sad farewell, camping in tents and wagons on the other shore, not knowing where it would be their lot to dwell—But He who hears the ravens when they cry, watched o'er the Camps of Israel, guided their ways, and, if they called for help, was ever nigh.

— *EMMELINE B. WELLS

A thousand unseen hands reach down to help you to their peace-crowned heights, and all the forces of the Firmament shall fortify your strength. Be not afraid to thrust aside half-truths and grasp the whole!

— ELLA WHEELER WILCOX

In these days of doubt and unbelief, it is very necessary that the children of the Latter-day Saints should be searching for convincing proof of the religion which their parents profess . . . many in the world would gladly believe in the faith of the Latter-day Saints, for they feel that we are in possession of peace and happiness, which they know not of; but they, through unbelief in a God who hears and answers prayers, refuse to call upon Him in humility as James the Apostle advised—to "prove all things, and hold fast that which is good."

— *LILLIE FREEZE

Hope is like the sun, which, as we journey toward it, casts the shadow of our burden behind us.

— SANDRA SMILES

Will you, at the very onset, subject the cause of Christ to ridicule by your own unwise and improper conduct? You are even more unreasonable than the children of Israel were . . . Where is your faith? Where is your confidence in God? Can you not realize that all things were made by him, and that he rules over all the works of his hands? And suppose that all the Saints here should lift their hearts in prayer to God, that the way might be opened before us, how easy it would be for him to cause the ice to break away, so that in a moment we could be on our journey!

— *LUCY MACK SMITH

If faith produces no works, I see that faith is not a living tree: thus faith and works together grow; no separate life they e'er can know; they're soul and body, hand and heart—what God hath joined, let no man part.

— HANNAH MORE

The Great Eternal of Eternity, thou God of Abraham, I look to thee; thou Omnipresent One, incline thy ear, and me, a child of dust, vouchsafe to hear.

— *ELIZA R. SNOW

Build a little fence of trust around today: fill each space with loving work and therein stay: look not through the sheltering bars upon tomorrow—God will help thee bear what comes of Joy or Sorrow.

— MARY FRANCES BUTTS

How strange it seems that I am so old. Still I do not *feel* old. It seems to me my morning of life has just dawned, there is so much in life to live for, so much to accomplish. Hope beams brightly— and energy is strong, and by the aid of my Heavenly Father I hope to make my life one of usefulness upon the earth.

— *DR. ELLIS REYNOLDS SHIPP

# Friendship

The only rose without thorns is Friendship.

— MLLE. DE SCUDERI

Only solitary men know the full joys of friendship. Others have their family; but to a solitary and an exile his friends are everything.

— WILLA CATHER

We may talk together under the same roof for many years, yet never really meet; and two others at first speech are old friends.

— MARY CATHERWOOD

Friendship is certainly the finest balm for the pangs of disappointed love.

— JANE AUSTEN

Friendships are discovered rather than made.

— HARRIET BEECHER STOWE

What a delight to make friends with someone you have despised!

— COLETTE

O Friendship! of all things the most rare, and therefore most rare because most excellent; whose comforts in misery are always sweet, whose counsels in prosperity are ever fortunate.

— LILLY

For there is no friend like a sister,
in calm or stormy weather;
To cheer one on the tedious way,
to fetch one if one goes astray,
To lift one if one totters down . . .
to strengthen whilst one stands.

— CHRISTINA ROSSETTI

Friendship is no plant of hasty growth; tho' planted in esteem's deep fixed soil, the gradual culture of kind intercourse must bring it to perfection.

— JOANNA BAILLIE

We feed one another in rations, serve affection
measured to the minimum daily requirement,
the very acceptable least —
While love bursts the walls of our larder, wondering,
Amazed, why we are afraid to feast.

— *CAROL LYNN PEARSON

Kind deeds, kind thoughts, the love of God, doing good to our fellow creatures, and a great charity for the failings of humanity, should actuate our lives day by day. If we see a poor boy or girl, as the case may be, or one who is not quite up with the world, and feels that he or she is slighted, let us speak cheerful and comforting words, and make his or her life a little brighter if it is possible to so do.

— *LYDIA D. ALDER

I would suggest that Friendship be the theme
Highest and worthiest of the poet's fire;
'Tis guiltless of deceit or selfish scheme,
And will true sympathy of soul inspire;
Linking together the divinest part
Of man or woman in affection true,
It will elevate and purify the heart,
Imparting strength to bear life's journey through.

— *EMMELINE B. WELLS

Both within the family and without, our sisters hold up our mirrors: our images of who we are—and of who we can dare to become.

— ELIZABETH FISHEL

If I can stop one heart from breaking,
I shall not live in vain:
If I can ease one life the aching,
or cool one pain,
Or help one fainting robin
unto his nest again—
I shall not live in vain.

— EMILY DICKINSON

# LEARNING

The true order of learning should be: first, what is necessary; second, what is useful; and third, what is ornamental. To reverse this arrangement is like beginning to build at the top of the edifice.

— MRS. SIGOURNEY

What novelty is worth the sweet monotony where everything is known—and loved because it is known?

— GEORGE ELIOT

Literature is the province of imagination, and stories, in whatever guise, are meditations on life.

— PAULA FOX

With the gain of knowledge, connect the habit of imparting it. This increases mental wealth by putting it in circulation; and it enhances the value of knowledge to ourselves, not only in its depth, confirmation and readiness for use, but in that acquaintance with human nature, that self-command, and that reaction of moral training upon ourselves, which are above all price.

— MRS. SIGOURNEY

If you have knowledge, let others light their candles at it.

— MARGARET FULLER

Books are meat and medicine and flame and flight and flower, steel, stitch, cloud and clout, and drumbeats on the air.

— GWENDOLYN BROOKS

We need as we have never needed a campaign of education . . . we need a baptism of the right kind of literature, periodicals, and truth-carrying messages that will make the people of the nation and the rest of the world sit up and take notice. The colleges, universities, and high schools are the laboratory where truth must be demonstrated.

— WINIFRED WILLARD

As one grows older one is more impatient with subterfuges and shams generally. . . the world is so confused that the least one can do is to keep one's mental integrity and to hold honestly to such poor wisdom as one has been able to garner on the way.

— JANE ADDAMS

The desire of knowledge, like the thirst of riches, increases ever with the acquisition of it.

— MARY STERNE

We are often prophets to others, only because we are our own historians.

— MME. SWETCHINE

It is more important that I have at least an hour a day to read and study; this is thinking and praying time.

— MADELINE L'ENGLE

In bad weather, when I couldn't go outside, I used to sit on those stairs and extract a "Geographic" as carefully as if I were playing pick-up sticks, so I wouldn't bring the whole attic down on myself. Among the glossy pages of the magazines, I met up with pygmies and Balinese dancers, cities built on water, mountain peaks yet unscaled, desert people and people who lived amid eternal snow, dragonflies and anacondas. On those attic stairs in an old house that seemed always on the verge of collapse, I began to sense huge possibilities.

— PAULA FOX

Have just returned from the last lecture of the day. Dr. Hunt on the hystology of the nerves, truly interesting. The more I learn the more understandingly I can say, "we are beautifully and wonderfully made."

— *DR. ELLIS REYNOLDS SHIPP

'Tis God gives skill, but not without men's hands: He could not make Antonio Stradivari's violins without Antonio.

— GEORGE ELIOT

Mankind is always in the human predicament, and that is what people write about. A great work of the imagination is one of the highest forms of communication of truth that mankind has reached.

— MADELINE L'ENGLE

Any experience worth living through is worth writing about — the act of writing about it significantly affects the experience itself.

— ANNE MORROW LINDBERGH

There is nothing more valuable to progress than perseverance. Whenever you fail in your attempts to do any good thing, let your motto be—try again.

— MARY HOWITT

We read to find out who we are. What other people, real or imaginary, do and think and feel . . . is an essential guide to our understanding of what we ourselves are and may become.

— URSULA K. LEGUIN

The greatest gift is the passion for reading. It is cheap, it consoles, it distracts, it excites.

— ELIZABETH HARDWICK

Her eye, her ear, were tuning forks, burning glasses, which caught the minutest reflection or echo of a thought or feeling . . . she heard a deeper vibration, a kind of composite echo, of all that the writer said, and did not say.

— WILLA CATHER

Every true woman should make self a study, so that she can properly and wisely perform her mission. Happy is the man that hath learned to read himself more than all books, and hath so taken this lesson that he can never forget it.

— *MILLIE HEPPLER

My admiration of literature, especially of poetical literature, can never be subdued nor can it be extinguished but with life.

— ELIZABETH BARRETT BROWNING

We are called to help regenerate and redeem the world. We must toil and sacrifice that our children may enjoy, and as "knowledge is power," as fast as we gain the knowledge we will attain to the power—then will we find time and opportunity for the cultivation of woman's higher, purer, nobler self.

— *JOSEPHINE SPENCER

We do think in words, and the fewer words we know, the more restricted our thoughts. As our vocabulary expands, so does our power to think. If we limit and distort language, we limit and distort personality . . . A great painting, or symphony, or play doesn't diminish us, but enlarges us—and we, too, want to make our own cry of affirmation to the power of creation behind the universe.

— MADELINE L'ENGLE

As a pupil of Professor Maeser, how blessed was my life! Under his superior tutelage I realized a truly great blessing in sharing the immensity of his knowledge, his power to impart the wealth of his intelligence and superior wisdom to the world. He helped me to higher ideals in so many ways. Every moment in his presence seemed a benediction, so great was his spiritual influence, his intuitive uplift to all that was pure and divine.

— *DR. ELLIS REYNOLDS SHIPP

The cultivation of the mind is of the greatest importance. Whatever persons undertake to learn, they should never leave that lesson until it is fully understood and mastered. Nothing great in Life is achieved only at the expense of unremitted labor.

— *JULIA LINTON

# PRAYER

God dwells far off from us, but prayer brings him down to our earth, and links his power with our efforts.

— MME. DE GASPARIN

I have lived to thank God that all my prayers have not been answered.

— JEAN INGELOW

I desire no other evidence of the truth of Christianity than the Lord's prayer.

— MME. DESTAEL

So weak is man, so ignorant and blind, that did not God sometimes withhold in mercy what we ask, we should be ruined at our own request.

— HANNAH MORE

Human life is a constant want, and ought to be a constant prayer.

— SALLY OSGOOD

Pray in your soul as you hasten to your duty.

— *DR. ELLIS REYNOLDS SHIPP

One of the greatest victories of the Enemy has been the separation of the sacred and the secular, and placing them in opposition. All of creation is sacred . . . healing used to be looked on as a sacred calling . . . we have forgotten the Spirit. I believe in prayer, and I believe in miracles.

— MADELINE L'ENGLE

Fountain of mercy! whose pervading eye can look within and read what passes there, accept my thoughts for thanks; I have no words, my soul o'er-fraught with gratitude rejects the aid of language—Lord!—behold my heart.

— HANNAH MORE

Prayer is not necessarily in fluency of speech; it is not in painted imagery; it is not in deep thoughts; it is not in burning words—it is the wish of the heart—the expression of the soul.

— ANNA TEMPLE

Prayer is right in itself as the most powerful means of resisting sin and advancing in holiness. It is above all might—as everything is which has the authority of Scripture, the command of God, and the example of Christ.

— HANNAH MORE

For this I pray:
to love Thy will, Lord of the ardent heart;
to bid all selfishness, all sloth depart,
to share with gladness all Thou dost and art—
for this I pray.

— ALICE M. KYLE

Prayer is an unfailing source of happiness. There can be no spiritual vitality about a man or a woman who does not pray; they know nothing about the power of their religion.

— *SUSA YOUNG GATES

I had an early run in the woods before the dew was off the grass. A very strange and solemn feeling came over me as I stood there . . . it seemed as if I *felt* God as I never did before, and I prayed in my heart that I might keep that happy sense of nearness all my life.

— LOUISA MAY ALCOTT

Heaven holds out the blessing like a bright, ripe fruit, only waiting for us to ask it: our words weave the basket.

— *CAROL LYNN PEARSON

I sought my Father and my God! He it was who inspired me with the higher intelligence, helped me to know my duty in all of its details, enabled me to run and not be weary, to walk and not faint. And with these same principles I tutored all who sought usefulness, enabling them to usher a new life into this world—that life so precious to the suffering mother, and most sublime in the sight of God. . . . I know 'twas not of me, but through the touch of One Divine, upon whose mighty arm I leaned.

— *DR. ELLIS REYNOLDS SHIPP

# VIRTUE AND WISDOM

Virtue is the habitual sense of right, and the habitual courage to act up to that sense of right.

— HARRIET BEECHER STOWE

Life is either a great adventure—or nothing at all.

— HELEN KELLER

Blessed is the memory of those who have kept themselves unspotted from the world! Yet more blessed and more dear the memory of those who have kept themselves unspotted *in* the world.

— MRS. JAMESON

Live virtuously, and you cannot die too soon, nor live too long.

— LADY RUSSELL

The chaste mind, like a polished plane, may admit foul thoughts, without receiving their tincture.

— LADY BLESSINGTON

The world stands out on either side
no wider than the heart is wide;
Above the world is stretched the sky—
no higher than the soul is high.
The heart can push the sea and land
farther away on either hand;
The soul can split the sky in two,
and let the face of God shine through.
But East and West will pinch the heart
that cannot keep them pushed apart;
And he whose soul is flat—the sky
will cave in on him, by and by.

— EDNA ST. VINCENT MILLAY

Impressive indeed, this shelf of books on which all the earth's critics dote. But oh, my son, how I wish that you had read the book I wrote.

— *CAROL LYNN PEARSON

No man can be wise on an empty stomach.

— GEORGE ELIOT

The first point of wisdom is to discern that which is false; the second, to know that which is true.

— HANNAH MORE

Our light must be burning, however dimly, and we must keep on the right road, however often we stumble on the way. Let us sit down before the Lord and count our resources, and see what we are fit for—let us decide honestly what we can do—and then do it with all our might.

— AMELIA E. BARR

Laugh, and the world laughs with you;
weep, and you weep alone,
For the sad old earth must borrow its mirth,
but has trouble enough of its own;
Feast, and your halls are crowded;
fast, and the world goes by,
Succeed and give, and it helps you live,
but no man can help you die.
There is room in the halls of pleasure
for a long and lordly train,
But one by one we must all file on
through the narrow isles of pain.

— ELLA WHEELER WILCOX

Certain springs are tapped only when we are alone. The artist knows he must be alone to create; the writer, to work out his thoughts; the musician, to compose; the saint, to pray. Women need solitude in order to find again the true essence of themselves.

— ANNE MORROW LINDBERGH

You may close the door upon me
and think, when you are gone,
"Poor thing, she's stuck at home all day."
How wrong, my dear, how wrong.
I am queen of my own castle,
I hold expectant sway,
For I decree what things will fill
the hours of my day. . . .
I've clothes to mend and tears to dry,
toys strewn across my floor,
But I have children's laughter, too,
and who could ask for more?
You come home to me, dear,
tired, from a world that is cold;
But I have angel lips to kiss,
and golden heads to hold,
And little arms about my neck,
and whispers in my ear:
Your world outside my castle wall
can't hold such treasures, dear.

— *SUSAN EVANS MCCLOUD

Talent and worth are the only eternal grounds of distinction. To these the Almighty has affixed his everlasting patent of nobility. Knowledge and goodness—these make degrees in heaven.

— MISS SEDGWICK

It is not popular to be willing to admit to sin. There appears to be a general misconception that if we admit to sin, then we are wallowing in it . . . but freedom and lightness follow when we say "I'm sorry," and are forgiven. It is equally unpopular to say, "I can't do it myself" . . . but Jesus of Nazareth always said, "I don't do this. It is my Father speaking through me." . . . Occasionally we are given the grace to turn away from our own image and toward God's image in us—and we have the model for this image in Jesus Christ.

— MADELINE L'ENGLE

Purity is the feminine, truth the masculine, of honor.

— INID HARE

Sin and licence always come first with honeyed promises of personal freedom. They sneak in masked as liberty, shaking their bells merrily, since, if we saw their faces, we would bar our doors as we would against the four horsemen themselves. . . . There is only one freedom—knowing and obeying God, by whatever name you may call him. There is no freedom but in knowing and living the truth. No soul is free until it has put under its feet the world, and the things of the world. There has never been but one Man big enough to be a free soul on this earth—and that man was a carpenter in Nazareth before he was tempted in all points, like as we are, and came forth free from sin—because he had conquered sin.

— ADELA ROGERS ST. JOHN

Nobility, without virtue, is a fine setting without a gem.

— JANE PORTER

Gradually I got used to the silence and the darkness that surrounded me, and forgot that it had ever been different . . . during the first nineteen months of my life I had caught glimpses of broad green fields, a luminous sky, trees and flowers which the darkness that followed could not wholly blot out. If we have once seen—"the day is ours, and what the day has shown."

— HELEN KELLER

# MERRIMENT:

## *To Lighten the Way*

If thou art merry, praise the Lord with singing,
with music, with dancing . . .
And with a prayer of praise & thanksgiving.

— D&C 136:28

The life that has grown up and developed without laughter, and without the sunny brightness which youth justly claims as its right, lacks buoyancy and elasticity, and becomes heavy and unsympathetic, if not harsh and morose.

— MRS. G. S. REANY

We do not please God more by eating bitter aloes than by eating honey . . . a funeral march is not so much like the music of angels as the songs of birds on a May morning . . . the great Christian graces are radiant with happiness. Faith, hope, charity—there is no sadness in them . . . God himself dwells in the light of joy as well as of purity.

— REBECCA DALE

If my heart were not light, I would die.

— JOANNA BAILLIE

An ounce of cheerfulness is worth a pound of sadness to serve God with.

— LOUISA MAY ALCOTT

God is glorified, not by our groans, but by our thanksgivings; and all good thought and good action claim a natural alliance with good cheer.

— ELIZABETH WHIPPLE

One of the greatest weapons of all is laughter — a gift for fun, a sense of play.

— MADELINE L'ENGLE

Be cheerful: do not brood over fond hopes unrealized until a chain is fastened on each thought and wound around the heart. Nature intended you to be the fountain-spring of cheerfulness and social life, and not the monument of despair and melancholy.

— ANNE HELPS

Not having enough sunshine is what ails the world.—Make people happy, and there will not be half the quarreling, or a tenth part of the wickedness there now is.

— LAURA CHILD

Look now! behold that wilderness, it blossoms as the rose, and smiling fields and orchards bloom in spite of all our foes. There's thousands now of happy homes, where peace and love abide, I think that we can fairly boast of Utah with great pride. Fair Utah, how I love that name! With joy my heart doth swell, and praise the Lord that I have been permitted there to dwell!

— *HATTIE J. HIGGINSON

Always look out for the sunlight the Lord sends into your days.

— HOPE CAMPBELL

By desiring what is perfectly good, even when we do not quite know what it is, and cannot do what we would, we are part of the divine power against evil, widening the skirts of light—and making the struggle with darkness narrower.

— GEORGE ELIOT

I have longings for more eyes. There is so much to see in this world all about.

— OPAL WHITELEY

I will be the gladdest thing under the sun! I will touch a hundred flowers, and not pick one!

— EDNA ST. VINCENT MILLAY

Invisible beauty has a word so brief, a flower can say it, or a shaken leaf . . . but few may ever snare it in a song.

— GRACE HAZARD CONKLING

Doubt no more that Oberon—
never doubt that Pan
Lived, and played a reed, and ran
after nymphs in a dark forest,
In the merry, credulous days,—lived,
and led a fairy band
Over the indulgent land!
Ah, for in this dourest, sorest age
men's eye has looked upon,
Death to fauns and death to fays,
still the dog-wood dares to raise—
Healthy tree, with trunk and root—
ivory bowls that bear no fruit,
And the starlings and the jays—
birds that cannot even sing—
Dare to come again in spring!

— EDNA ST. VINCENT MILLAY

You hear that boy laughing? You think he's all fun:
But the angels laugh, too, at the good he has done.

— NORAH HOLLAND

Today I have grown taller from walking with the trees.

— KARLE WILSON

I'll walk where my own nature would be leading—
It vexes me to choose another guide—
Where the grey flocks in ferny glens are feeding,
Where the wild wind blows on the mountain-side.

— EMILY BRONTË

I know the Christ on whose name I call was creating galaxies and snowflakes long before there were living beings naming the animals in the Garden. Perhaps the morning stars still sing together, only we have forgotten the language.

— MADELINE L'ENGLE

The mad, merry music, that set us a-dancing,
Till over the midnight came stealing the morn.

— NORA PERRY

Hang up the baby's stocking;
be sure you don't forget
The dear little dimpled darling!
She's ne'er seen Christmas yet.

— EMILY HUNTINGTON MILLER

Spring rides no horses down the hill, but comes on foot,
A goose girl still.
And all the loveliest things there be come simply, so
It seems to me.

— EDNA ST. VINCENT MILLAY

I think that folk should carry bright umbrellas in the rain,
To smile into the sullen sky, and make it glad again.

— MARGARET E. SANGSTER

There's nothing half so pleasant as coming home again!

— MRS. GERRIT VANDETH

Talk happiness. The world is sad enough without your woe—No path is wholly rough.

— ELLA WHEELER WILCOX

We shall walk in velvet shoes: wherever we go
Silence will fall like dews on white silence below . . .
We shall walk in the snow.

— ELINOR HOYT WYLIE

Let me grow lovely, growing old—
so many fine things do:
Laces and ivory and gold,
and silks need not be new.

— KARLE WILSON

I love it, I love it; and who shall dare to chide me for loving that old armchair?

— ELIZA COOK

The day before April alone, alone,
I walked to the woods and sat on a stone.
I sat on a broad stone and sang to the birds.
The tune was God's making, but I made the words.

— MARY CAROLYN DAVIES

I have an understanding with the hills . . . at evening when the slanted radiance fills their hollows, and the great winds let them be, and they are quiet, and look down at me.

— GRACE HAZARD CONKLING

I meant to do my work today—
But a brown bird sang in the apple-tree,
and a butterfly flitted across the field,
and all the leaves were calling me.
And the wind went sighing over the land,
tossing the grasses to and fro,
And a rainbow held out its shining hand—
so what could I do but laugh and go?

— MARY LESLIE NEWTON

Spend all you have for loveliness,
Buy it and never count the cost;
For one white singing hour of peace
Count many a year of strife well lost,
And for a breath of ecstasy
Give all you have been, or could be.

— SARA TEASDALE

The swallows are gone and the golden rod has given way to Astors. Even some hasty Maples are donning Fall colours to keep up with the season. We've had a slight, light frost, too, and the crickets are in full chorus. The Dipper is low in the Northern sky of an evening and the stars are glittery. *And* the eight cords of firewood are all stacked and in. . . . Tea is enjoyable by the fire now, and bare feet feel chilly. I long to sew winter frocks and red petticoats! And knitting after breakfast for half an hour is back in style—Delightful!

— TASHA TUDOR

Some days my thoughts are just cocoons—
all cold and dull and blind,
They hang from dripping branches
in the gray woods of my mind;
And other days they drift and shine—
such free and flying things!
I find the gold-dust in my hair,
left by their brushing wings!

— KARLE WILSON BAKER

New Year—bring us success and happiness. Bring us sunshine and prosperity. Bring us strength to keep our resolves, that our characters may be emblems of goodness, holiness, and purity. And while we forever worship and sing praises to our Heavenly Father, the great Giver of all blessings, yet we should cry with hearts of cheer—louder and louder, a welcome to 1894—until the echoes resound from the far distant snowy-topped mountain peaks, with a sweet but faint reply of *Welcome! Welcome! Welcome!*

— *ANNIE SMITH

When she was giving more wash-outs to the clothes that did fall, she did sing. She sings on days when sunshine is. She sings on days when rain is. Sadie McKibben always sings before the summer rain, as does the robin.

— OPAL WHITELEY

I am like the grass of the fields: water and sun, that is all I need. I have just come from playing with my little children. They are so dear, and my big children are so good to me, that I shall die, I believe, smiling at them.

— GEORGE SAND (AURORA DUPIN)

The orderlies and cleaning women love her; whenever there has been a crisis in her condition there have been tears, open and unashamed . . . perhaps she is being kept here on Earth for so long because her gift of laughter is desperately needed . . .

— MADELINE L'ENGLE

It is in those acts which we call trivialities that the seeds of joy are forever wasted.

— GEORGE ELIOT

When troubles come from God, then naught behoves like patience; but for troubles wrought of men, patience is hard—I tell you, it is hard.

— JEAN INGELOW

Ah! If you only knew the peace there is in an accepted sorrow.

— MME. GUION

Outward attacks and troubles rather fix than unsettle the Christian, As tempests from without only serve to root the oak faster; while an inward canker will gradually rot and decay it.

— HANNAH MORE

The only way to meet affliction is to pass through it solemnly, slowly, with humility and faith, as the Israelites passed through the sea. Then its very waves of misery will divide, and become to us a wall, on the right side, and on the left, until the gulf narrows before our eyes—and we see land safe on the opposite shore.

— MISS MULOCK

Paradoxical as it may seem, God means not only to make us good, but to make us also happy—by sickness, disaster, and disappointments.

— CAROL PARKER

If your cup seems too bitter, if your burden seems too heavy, be sure that it is the wounded hand that is holding the cup—and that it is He who carries the cross that is carrying the burden.

— MRS. POWELL

Strength is born in the deep silence of long-suffering hearts—not amid joy.

— MRS. HEMANS

The true way of softening one's troubles is to solace those of others.

— MME. DE MAINTENON

Our Heavenly Father has gone through the learning process himself. He has a profound understanding of what we have to do. He has a goal for us. He wants us to all return to him, but he nowhere says that we all have to be the same to do that . . . There is no waste, and there is no haste. We will have all the time we need. We have a loving Father who makes sure we will receive the experiences we need to achieve perfection. He will let us start over again as often as we need to.

—*CHIEKO N. OKAZAKI

This evening I fully expected my husband here, but was again disappointed. . . . He is not in want of me for a companion or in any sense, he does not need me at all. There are plenty ready and willing to administer to every wish, caprice or whim of his, indeed they anticipate them, they are near him always, while I am shut out of his life. . . . It is impossible for me to make myself useful to him in any way while I am held at such a distance.

— *EMMELINE B. WELLS

Strength alone knows conflict; weakness is below even defeat, and is born vanquished.

— MME. SWETCHINE

To those leaning on the sustaining Infinite, today is big with blessings.

— MARY BAKER EDDY

No affliction would trouble a child of God if he knew God's reasons for sending it.

— WINIFRED WILLARD

Like the winds of the sea are the ways of fate;
As the voyage along through life:
'Tis the will of the soul that decides its goal—
And not the calm or the strife.

— ELLA WHEELER WILCOX

They did not in their trials draw out from the springs of consolation that which the gospel presents—that support which was their privilege, and which would have enabled them to rejoice in the midst of tribulation and disappointment.

— *ELIZA R. SNOW

Above all that I can remember of my life in St. Louis is that we were horribly, horribly poor . . . we seldom had all that we could eat or enough clothes to wear . . . There were times when Mother used to send me to the home of a neighbor, a darling old German woman, for a nickel so that she could take a car downtown to see if my father had given a dance lesson that day. A lesson meant that we could have some supper. God gave me one jewel in life beyond price: my mother—whose faith and courage gave me hope and the will to endure failure, and whose love and affection have been my rewards for what success I may have achieved in my work.

— LAURA LAPLANTE

If Heavenly Father can heal at all—then He can heal all. The most unspeakable nightmarish atrocities will, with his touch, pass away, and even the memory of them will have no power to mar our wholeness and joy.

— *SUSAN EVANS MCCLOUD

Build on resolve, and not upon regret, the structure of the future. Do not grope among the shadows of old sins, but let thine own soul's light shine on the path of hope, and dissipate the darkness.

— ELLA WHEELER WILCOX

Listen, children: your father is dead.
From his old coats I'll make you little jackets;
I'll make you little trousers from his old pants.
There'll be in his pockets things he used to put there,
Keys and pennies covered with tobacco;
Dan shall have the pennies to save in his bank;
Anne shall have the keys to make a pretty noise with.
Life must go on, though good men die;
Anne, eat your breakfast; Dan, take your medicine;
Life must go on; I forget just why.

— EDNA ST. VINCENT MILLAY

To fight aloud is very brave, but gallanter, I know,
Who charge within the bosom the cavalry of woe.

— EMILY DICKINSON

When all is beautiful, and bright and fair, and tranquil flows the pleasant stream of life, we may forget its sorrow, toil, or care, Perchance e'en bitterness, and pain and strife. Some precious lessons trials may have taught; we may be purer, wiser, and more just; Some beauty in our souls may have been wrought through faith in God, obedience and trust.

— *EMMELINE B. WELLS

We had only one decent dress at a time, so we had to go to bed early Saturday night so Mother could wash not only our dresses, but all our underwear too and dry it through the night, that we might be clean for Sunday. But I never remember hearing my mother complain.

— *SABRA JANE BECKSTEAD

Visited the sick yesterday. I cooked for the widow and orphan and poor, that they might feast and have their hearts made glad today in the counsel house.

— *PATTY BARTLETT SESSIONS

Build for yourself a strong-box,
fashion each part with care;
When it's strong as your hand can make it,
put all your troubles there;
Hide there all thought of your failures,
and each bitter cup that you quaff;
Lock all your heartaches within it,
then sit on the lid and laugh.

— BERTHA ADAMS BACHUS

Brother, wherefore art thou fearful?
Sister, why this dread of ill?
He who succored ancient Israel lives,
and loves His children still.
Cling to Him with trust unshaken,
every blessing waits for you;
All his words are full of promise—
all His promises are true.

— *LULU GREENE RICHARDS

We got into a room, partly underground and partly on top of the ground . . . my husband broke (out) in sores all over his body, so that you could not put a pin point on him without putting it on a sore, from the crown of his head to the soles of his feet . . . we had one spoonful of sugar and one saucer full of cornmeal, so I made mush . . . and gave it to my children. We were in a strange land among strangers. The conflict began in my mind: *"Your folks told you your husband would be killed, and are you not sorry that you did not listen to them?"* I said, *"No, I am not. I did what was right. If I die, I am glad I was baptized . . ."* After that a third person spoke. It was a still, small voice this time saying, *"Hold on, for the Lord will provide."* I said I would, for I would trust in Him and not grumble.

— *DRUSILLA DORRIS HENDRICKS

My heart is too susceptible of sorrow. It breaks down beneath a burden that some would carry with ease.

— *DR. ELLIS REYNOLDS SHIPP

Sin and cruelty, and falsehood we can avoid, if we will; sickness, poverty, and death are beyond our control. We must bear and forebear.

— *M.A.Y. GREENHALGH

Sometime, when all life's lessons have been learned,
And sun and stars forevermore have set,
The things which our weak judgments here have spurned—
The things o'er which we grieved with lashes wet—
Will flash before us out of life's dark night,
As stars shine most in deeper tints of blue;
And we shall see how all God's plans were right,
And how what seemed reproof was love most true.

— *MARY E. CONNELLY

The brave man is not he who feels no fear, for that were stupid and irrational; but he whose noble soul subdues its fear, and bravely dares the danger nature shrinks from.

— JOANNA BAILLIE

Lizzie much worse. A hard thing to hear; but if she is only to suffer, I pray she may go soon. . . Sad, quiet days in her room, and strange nights watching the dear little shadow try to wile away the long sleepless hours without troubling me . . . so sweet and patient, and so worn, my heart is broken to see the change . . . For two days she suffered much—Tuesday she lay in Father's arms, smiling contentedly, as she held our hands and kissed us tenderly . . . So the first break comes, and I know what death means—A liberator for her, a teacher for us.

— LOUISA MAY ALCOTT

I slept and dreamed that life was beauty,
I woke—and found that Life was duty;
Was my dream, then, a shadowy lie?
Toil on, sad heart, courageously,
And thou shalt find thy dreams shall be
A noonday light and truth to thee.

— ELLEN STURGIS HOOPER

Great minds are they who suffer not in vain. Oh, I would hope I have suffered not in vain . . . I do not feel my spirit great. But oh, I have suffered—and I pray it has never been in vain.

— *DR. ELLIS REYNOLDS SHIPP

I had for a long time braced every nerve, roused every energy of my soul and called upon God to strengthen me, but when I entered the room and saw my murdered sons extended both at once before my eyes . . . I sank back, crying to the Lord in the agony of my soul . . . Oh! at that moment how my mind flew through every scene of sorrow and distress we had passed, together, in which they had shown the innocence and sympathy which filled their guileless hearts. As I looked upon their peaceful, smiling countenances, I seemed almost to hear them say, *"Mother, weep not for us, we have overcome the world by love . . . they slew us for our testimony, and thus placed us beyond their power; their ascendency is for a moment, ours is an eternal triumph."*

— *LUCY MACK SMITH

When I look at her pictures, of her as an old woman, I am humbled by the serenity and joy in her face. There is never a trace of bitterness or resentment, and she had much cause for both. I see only quiet strength, silent endurance.

— MADELINE L'ENGLE

I will have nothing to do with a God who cares only occasionally. I need a God who is with us always, everywhere, in the deepest depths as well as the highest heights. It is when things go wrong, when the good things do not happen, when our prayers seem to have been lost—that God is most present.

— MADELINE L'ENGLE